Nana's Bible Stories

Roberta Simpson

ILLUSTRATED BY SUSAN MITCHELL

FOREWORD BY SARAH FERGUSON
THE DUCHESS OF YORK

NANA'S BIBLE STORIES

Published in Nashville, Tennessee, by Thomas Nelson, Inc.

Library of Congress Cataloging-in-Publication Data

Simpson, Roberta.
  Nana's Bible stories / by Roberta Simpson.
     p. cm.
  Summary: "Basic Bible stories told in easy to understand language"--Provided by publisher.
  ISBN-13: 978-1-4003-1070-8 (Jane Seymour audio)
  ISBN-10: 1-4003-1070-9 (Jane Seymour audio)
  ISBN-13: 978-1-4003-1187-3 (Sheila Walsh audio)
  ISBN-10: 1-4003-1187-X (Sheila Walsh audio)
  1. Bible stories, English. I. Title.
BS551.3.S57 2007
220.9'505--dc22
                          2007009293

Printed in China
07 08 09 HH 9 8 7 6 5 4 3 2 1

Since I was a young girl, reading books has been my favorite hobby. As I grew, I began to make up stories, eventually telling these stories to my own children. They always seemed to enjoy my stories more than those we read in books.

Years later, I became a "Nana," and family and friends continued to encourage my storytelling. One day after baby-sitting two of my grandchildren, a friend asked me what "crazy story" I had made up for them. After telling her about my story of Jesus and the little lost lamb—complete with exciting lions, bears, and wolves—she challenged me to have Nana's stories published. Initially, I had no interest in the possibility of a publisher rejecting my stories. As I got in my car to leave, however, I felt the Lord impressing upon me, "You can NOW write." I am glad that God is so merciful! I could not wait to get home to write down my stories!

At the age of seventy, I was not looking to establish a career, so I am in awe at what the Lord has done. There are no words to express the joy in my heart as I write my "stories within Bible stories." I pray that through *Nana's Bible Stories* children will see and grow to love the "real" Jesus, who came and dwelt among men, and who loved all children with extreme passion!

I want to thank my children and my wonderful husband, Kyffin Simpson, who have encouraged me from the beginning. I would also like to express my deep appreciation to Rich Marshall for taking the time to read my first story and to Pastor Steve Hill who truly blessed me in many ways—including introducing me to my colleague and new friend, Nancy Delmar.

I dedicate this book to my grandchildren—Raphael, Netanya, Nathan, Alexandra, Samuel, Kyffin, Solomon, Sophia, and Charlie, who are my inspiration.

Also, to my Lord and Savior, Jesus Christ—Yeshua, without whom there would be no stories!

Nana

My dear friend, Roberta Simpson, has a true gift for storytelling. For years, I have witnessed how she has captivated parents and children alike with her imaginative and engaging tales.

Roberta transports the reader back in time through her vivid imagery and attention to detail that make her characters and storylines come alive. Indeed even the most familiar stories from the Bible are presented in a fresh, new way through Roberta's Mother Goose–like character, "Nana."

A beautiful and vibrant woman, Roberta is an inspiration to all as she embarks on her writing career at the age of seventy. She is motivated by her passion for children and desire to make a difference in the lives of those in need.

Toward that end, Roberta will generously donate a portion of proceeds from the sale of Nana's Bible Stories to charities benefiting young people.

I believe people of all ages will treasure Roberta's book as much as I do.

Sarah Ferguson

Table of Contents

A Giant Man vs. A Giant Faith

Can you imagine coming face-to-face with a giant?
It would probably be more like "face-to-waist," since the giant would be at least
twice your height! And just imagine how big his hands and feet would be!

I have never seen a giant, but I know a true story about a giant who lived
thousands of years ago. He was mean and horrible, and everyone was very
afraid of him—everyone but a boy named David.

Aaron was shivering with fright and cold. It was early morning, and he could hear that terrible giant, Goliath, shouting horrible insults about the Israelites. His voice was so loud that it shook the ground. Aaron had watched the few men who tried to stand up to him; they had all run away in terror when the giant drew his sword.

Aaron was no soldier. He was only a helper who brought water to the soldiers and cleaned their sandals and swords.

"When is someone brave going to come and kill this giant?" he would ask himself each day.

Aaron thought about the green hills near his home, the flocks of sheep, and his friend, David. Often, David would play his harp and sing songs about God. Just listening to those songs had strengthened Aaron's faith. But now, he was homesick, lonely, and afraid.

Just then, he heard someone call his name. "Aaron, is that you?" Aaron could not believe his ears! He looked up to see David running toward him.

"My dad sent me to bring food to my brothers," David said.

"I know just where they are," replied Aaron, smiling now. "Follow me!"

David looked around excitedly as they entered the Israelite camp. He caught sight of the battlefield. "Wow . . ." He grinned at Aaron. "I can't believe I am really here. This is *very* different from minding my father's sheep."

They could still hear Goliath shouting insults to the army of Israel. As David and Aaron walked among the soldiers, they could feel the fear in the air.

Aaron whispered to David, "I don't think anyone is going to fight that giant."

David couldn't believe it. "Who does this pagan think he is anyway, going against the armies of the living God? Don't the soldiers know that our God is stronger than this giant?"

King Saul was in his beautiful tent, sitting on a carved, wooden throne and surrounded by all his generals and advisors, when he sent for David. David entered confidently, saying, "Your Majesty, don't worry about this Philistine giant. I will go and fight him!"

King Saul's eyes widened in amazement at David's boldness. "Don't be ridiculous! There is *no way* you can fight this Philistine and win! You are only a boy, and he has been fighting since his youth!"

King Saul turned to walk away, but David cried out, "I have been taking care of my father's sheep and goats. When a wild animal comes to steal a lamb, I go after it with a club and rescue the lamb from the animal's mouth. I have killed lions and bears, and I'll kill this giant too, because he has spoken against the army of God! The Lord who rescued me from the claws of the lion and the bear will rescue me from this Philistine."

King Saul sighed and turned back. "What other option do I have?"
He motioned for servants to give his own armor and spear to David.

Aaron was so proud of his friend. But when David put on the king's
armor, he collapsed in a heap on the floor. Aaron had to put his hand
over his mouth to muffle his laughter. As David crawled out from under
the heavy armor, he turned to King Saul. "Oh, King, I can't wear your
armor. I have to fight the giant my way."

"Come and help me choose five good stones," David said to Aaron as
they walked from Saul's tent to a little stream nearby. Then, armed with
nothing more than his sling, five stones, and a shepherd's staff, David
marched bravely onto the battlefield.

When he saw David, Goliath sneered with disgust at the handsome, young boy. "Do you think I'm just a dog that you can fight with a stick?" He yelled ugly things at David. Then he roared, "Come over here, and I'll give your body to the birds and wild animals!"

Watching, Aaron became worried. He prayed, "Dear God, please help David. Goliath looks so strong, and David looks so small. But I know you are stronger than anyone. Please help David win the battle!"

To the amazement of the Israelite soldiers, David didn't run away. He said to Goliath, "You come to me with a sword, spear, and javelin, but I come to you in the name of the Lord—the God of the armies of Israel, whom you have been insulting. Today the Lord will defeat you, and the whole world will know that there is a God in Israel. And everyone who is here will know that the Lord rescues his people, but not with a sword and spear. This is *the Lord's* battle, and he will give you to us!"

David reached into his shepherd's bag and took out a stone. Just as Aaron had seen David do a dozen times, he swung the sling in a tight circle and sent a stone flying through the air, straight toward Goliath. As the stone found its mark in Goliath's forehead, the giant's head snapped back. The air was deathly still as the giant toppled slowly, like a tree cut with an ax.

Aaron felt the ground shake as Goliath's body hit the dirt, sending a cloud of dust into the air. Then the field was no longer silent. The sound of thousands of pounding feet filled Aaron's ears as the rest of the Philistines ran away. The Israelite soldiers let out loud cheers of victory, grabbed their weapons, and gave chase.

Oh, the rejoicing that was in the camp that day! Aaron called to David, "I knew you could do it!"

David laughed and shook his head. "I knew *God* could do it!"

Aaron nodded and sent up a silent prayer. *God, you won the battle for him. Thank you!*

How do you think David felt after defeating that big giant?
Do you believe God will help us fight our battles no matter what they are?

David had faith. What is faith? Faith is trusting God completely.
Even if our faith is very small, each time we use it, it grows even bigger!

You can be a mighty person like David.
Just put your faith in God and live to please him!

If you would like to read more about this story in the Bible, go to 1 Samuel 17.

A Father's Miracle

A miracle is when God does something that nothing and no one else could do, such as healing someone from a terrible sickness or disease. In our story, Nathan's father had an awful disease called leprosy. In biblical times, everyone who had the disease died. But God had a miracle in store for Nathan's family.

The boy in our story is named Nathan, which means "gift from God."

There are four other Hebrew words I'd like to teach you:

Yahweh (pronounced YAH-weh) means God

Yeshua (pronounced YAY-shu) means Jesus

Abba (pronounced AB-uh) means Daddy

Ima (pronounced EE-ma) means Mother

Nathan's family lived in a small, neat house near the lake. Every day, after finishing his schoolwork, Nathan would rush into his dad's woodshop and do all kinds of handy things for his dad. He loved to watch his dad take a piece of wood and make it into something beautiful or useful. His father's hands were big and rough, but they could produce such smooth, delicate things.

Many times after a hard day working with wood, Nathan and his dad would go down to the lake where they fished and talked for hours. They would return home, carrying fish for supper, their clothes smelling of sawdust and river mud.

One particular day, Nathan's dad was making a beautiful table for a lady who lived nearby. "Abba, I just love this table!" Nathan exclaimed. "I wish we could keep it."

His dad smiled. "Your mother would love to have one," he replied. "But right now, we need the money that this table will bring."

After a while, they heard Mother calling them for dinner. As Nathan's dad washed his hands, Nathan noticed the water turning red. "Abba!" he cried out. "You must have cut yourself!"

"Hmm, I didn't feel anything." His dad looked puzzled.

At dinner, Father gave a blessing over the meal and thanked Yahweh for a wonderful day. The family talked and laughed and told stories of the wonderful things that Yahweh had done for their people. When it was time for bed, Nathan's dad said a prayer and blessed each member of the family.

"I am so lucky," Nathan told his parents as they blew out the candle. "I don't know what I would do if something ever happened to you."

"Our trust is in Yahweh, and he will take care of us," his mother answered with a smile and a kiss.

His father's hand got worse. The cut looked sore and ugly and the bandages had to be changed often. Nathan's parents looked worried and very sad.

One afternoon, Nathan found his mother crying quietly and his dad trying to comfort her.

His dad wiped the tears from his mother's face. "Son, we have bad news. I have to go away," Nathan's dad began.

Nathan filled with panic. "No, Abba, no!" he cried. "You can't leave us! Why?"

Nathan's dad put his good hand on Nathan's head. "I have leprosy. The priest confirmed it today. Because it is so catching, our law says I cannot be around other people." His dad knelt down and looked him in the eyes. "You must help your mother. The table for our neighbor is ready, and the money will feed you for a long time."

Nathan had seen people with leprosy before. They wore rags to cover the sores on their faces and hands. They smelled awful, and cried out, "Unclean! Unclean!" to warn anyone who came near them. Nathan could not believe his own Abba would become like that.

The family clung together as Abba prepared to leave. Would they ever be a family again?

"Pray for a miracle." Nathan's father looked deeply into his eyes. "Only Yahweh can heal me." With that, Nathan's father turned and walked toward the edge of town. Nathan watched him grow farther and farther away, until he could no longer see his father through his tears.

Can you imagine how you would feel if you were Nathan?
What would you do?
I imagine there were many tears in Nathan's home that night.

As Mother tucked the children into their beds, she whispered to each one of them, "Pray for a miracle . . . pray for a miracle."

How could Yahweh let this happen? Nathan wondered. Then, he remembered the story of Yahweh parting the Red Sea. Healing his father seemed like such a little miracle compared to that. Nathan promised himself that he would pray every day until his dad came home.

Months went by and Nathan was soothed by his mother's words: "Yahweh will take care of us." And indeed he had. The money for the table had come just in time. But what would happen when that money was gone?

At the edge of town, Nathan's dad was getting worse. Sores covered his body. He wished for his family and his home. He missed the smile of his wife and hugs from his children. He was afraid and sick and so lonely.

One day, he heard about someone performing miracles in Galilee. The deaf were hearing, the blind were seeing, and this man Yeshua was the reason for it all. Many people said he was the promised Messiah.

Nathan's dad set out toward Galilee. It was hot and he had to avoid traveling near anyone on the road. When evening approached, he saw a crowd of people as they caught sight of him. With looks of horror and disgust, some shouted, "Unclean!" before he could even get the words out. One man even picked up a rock and would have thrown it if Yeshua had not stopped him.

Instead of turning away, Yeshua walked toward Nathan's dad. Dropping to his knees, Nathan's dad knew in his heart that this was the person with the power to heal. With all his strength, he said to Jesus, "If you are willing, you can make me clean."

Never before had anyone looked at Nathan's dad with such love and compassion. Yeshua saw past the sores and knew him inside and out. Jesus touched him and said, "Of course I am willing! Be clean." He said it so powerfully, yet with such tenderness.

Nathan's dad shook with excitement! Yeshua had healed him! His skin was perfectly clear! Yeshua smiled at him and said, "Before you say anything, go to the priest; let him declare you healed."

But how could he keep quiet? He was so excited that he told everyone on his way to the priest, "Yeshua healed me! I can go home!"

In the small, neat house by the lake, Nathan finished his prayer as he always did. "And Yahweh, please heal Abba and bring him home." As he raised his head, he looked across the table. Mother always set a plate and spoon there for her husband, never giving up hope.

As Mother passed the bread, Nathan heard something. It came again, and this time they understood the words: "Is my family home?"

Could it really be their beloved Abba?! They all ran outside, and there he was—clean and well, with a huge smile on his face. What a reunion! They hugged him and kissed him, all crying tears of joy. Nathan's father was home!

Dinner got cold that night, and the children did not go to bed until their dad had told them everything. He told about being a lonely leper and of the man who had healed him. "It was Yeshua, the Messiah we've waited for—Yahweh's own Son."

Nathan went to bed happier than he had ever been. "I knew you would heal him, Yahweh. Thank you so much!" As he drifted to sleep, he thought of how amazing it was that God's own Son had given him back his father.

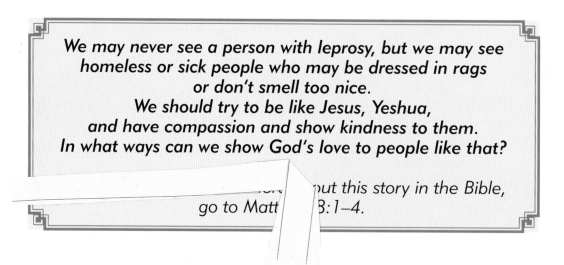

We may never see a person with leprosy, but we may see homeless or sick people who may be dressed in rags or don't smell too nice.
We should try to be like Jesus, Yeshua, and have compassion and show kindness to them.
In what ways can we show God's love to people like that?

...put this story in the Bible, go to Matt... 8:1–4.

A Donkey's Tale

Have you ever ridden a donkey? Donkeys have little, hard hooves that are great for gripping rocks. My grandchildren and I recently rode donkeys up some very steep cliffs. It was scary looking down over the cliffs, but it was great fun!

Today we are going to hear the story of a donkey that lived thousands of years ago. And I'm going to let you hear the story right from the donkey's mouth!

Hi, kids! I'm Nara, a donkey. I know you may be thinking, *A donkey? Why would I listen to a donkey?* Well, my owner, Balaam, once thought the very same thing. But he would soon realize that God had chosen me, a little donkey, to save his life.

Do you believe that God has a plan for our lives? Maybe you sometimes say, "I'm just a kid. . . ." At one time I thought, *I'm just a donkey.* But even though I am only a donkey, God was able to use me in a very unique and powerful way.

I was young when Balaam bought me. My job was to take my master wherever he wanted to go. Balaam was a prophet of God, but he was too fond of money. One time the king of Moab wanted to pay my master a lot of money to do a bad thing.

The king of Moab sent his princes to my master. They came on camels, richly dressed and bringing gifts. The camels were tied right beside me, but being camels belonging to princes, they wouldn't even look at me. I suppose I was lucky they didn't spit!

The king asked Balaam if he would curse God's people, the Israelites. (To curse someone is to ask God to do bad things to them.) At first Balaam said no. He would not pray for bad things to happen to God's people.

But, the next morning, Balaam got up and prepared me for a long journey. We had been traveling for a while, when all of a sudden, I stopped right in my tracks! There in front of me stood a large angel, with a very bright, long sword in his hand, blocking my way on the road.

Balaam started beating and kicking me to get me back on the road. It was as if my master hadn't seen anything, but I don't know how he could help seeing that angel! I think most angels are gentle, kind, and comforting, but this angel was not happy! I was going to stay as far away as I could from that angel.

We came to a narrow path between two vineyards. We had to pass between two walls, and when we did, there was the fierce angel standing in front of me again. Scared, I pressed close to the far wall to get away, and crushed my master's foot. His pain gave him new strength and he started to beat me all over again.

What could I do? The angel of the Lord stood in front of me with a flaming sword, and my master was beating and kicking me to make me go forward. I gave up. I sank down onto the ground with Balaam still on my back and refused to move.

Balaam was angrier than I had ever seen him. His face turned red and his eyes were wide like his whole head was about to explode! He started to beat me with his staff. It hurt! Oh, how I wanted to yell at him, to tell him about the angel, but he would never have understood my donkey language!

But all of a sudden, guess what? The Lord opened my mouth and I spoke. Imagine Balaam's shock when he heard his donkey say, "What have I done to you to make you beat me three times?"

I thought he would have fainted, hearing me talk! Much to my surprise, Balaam answered, "You have made a fool of me! If I had a sword in my hand, I would have killed you!"

I said, "But I am the same donkey you always ride on. Have I ever done this to you before?"

"Noooo," he answered, thinking.

At that moment, Balaam saw the angel for the first time. His face turned white, and his hands started to tremble. He slid from my back and threw himself face down into the dust of the road.

Then the angel *really* surprised me. He defended me—me, a donkey! Can you imagine? He said, "Why have you beaten your donkey these three times? I have come here to stop you because your path is a reckless one. The donkey saw me and turned away all three times. If she hadn't, I certainly would have killed you by now."

41

The angel and my master spoke for a while, and we went on to meet the king. This time we were going to do things *God's* way. After we arrived, Balaam gave that king a big surprise when he blessed the people of Israel instead of cursing them. You should have seen how mad the king of Moab was then!

But God was pleased that Balaam did the right thing.

I guess that just goes to show that God has a purpose for us all. Balaam had a purpose to bless God's people, and even I, a donkey, had a purpose to help Balaam do the right thing. Maybe you should talk to God about his purpose for *you*! Whatever it is, you can be sure God can make it happen—just ask a little donkey that talked!

You might be thinking, How can God use me? Well, in our story, God used a donkey! God loves you more than a million donkeys! No matter how small you feel, God cares for you and has big plans for your life. When you trust God and follow him, you'll be amazed at what he can do through you!!

If you want to read about the story of Balaam's donkey in the Bible, go to Numbers 22:21–38.

A Child Sees Jesus

Before we begin this next story, let's pretend for a moment. Close your eyes and imagine what it would be like if you were blind. How would you get dressed or find the bathroom? Today, blind people can live very active and happy lives. They can read books, work on computers, and special dogs are trained to help them live by themselves. But in Bible times, blind people were not as fortunate. They usually grew up to be beggars. Imagine how Levi felt, knowing what his future would hold. . . .

There was a great excitement in the village. Jesus was coming to town! Most had never seen him, but everyone had heard of him. Jesus, the one who had healed the sick, opened the eyes of the blind and the ears of the deaf, was actually coming to their village!

"Do you think we will see him?" Rebecca asked.

"I sure hope so," Levi said, rubbing his eyes. "Well, at least *you* could see him." Levi had been blind since an accident when he was only three years old.

Rebecca squeezed Levi's shoulder reassuringly. Six months ago, Rebecca had been dying of a terrible disease when Jesus had healed her. "He healed me. I just know he can heal you too."

Rebecca's mother, Rachel, watched the children through the window. Her mind wandered back to that day when Jesus had healed her daughter. She had run out of the house shouting, desperately trying to get the attention of this man, the Son of God, the one who healed. She smiled to herself as she recalled his smile—full of such love and understanding. She thought, *I do hope Jesus will heal Levi like he healed my Rebecca!*

When Rebecca came inside, she and her mom made a plan. They would round up the mothers and children in the village, and they would all go to Jesus together. The mothers became very excited. A touch from Jesus! Some wanted healing, but all wanted blessings for their little ones.

When the day came at last, the village awoke early. The parents prepared to take their children to Jesus, so that he would bless them. Everyone was busy. Delicious smells were coming from the houses, where women were busy baking yummy breads. Little girls put on their special dresses, and the boys allowed their mothers to wash behind their ears without a complaint.

The morning was almost over when someone shouted, "Look, a group of men are coming down the road! It must be Jesus and his disciples!"

At first the women and children held back a little, while the men went forward and started chatting. Jesus was so friendly! And his laugh—no one could resist laughing with him!

Rachel stood watching from a distance. Her heart started to thump. Would he remember them? She straightened her shoulders. It was not the custom for women to be so forward, but this was different, she told herself. She took Rebecca's hand and started walking toward Jesus, calling to the other mothers and children to follow.

Jesus turned, and when he saw Rebecca, he grinned, knelt, and opened his arms. Rebecca let go of her mother's hand and gave Jesus a huge hug.

"How are you, Rebecca? It is wonderful to see you again, happy and well!"

"I am just fine!" Rebecca said. "I have never felt better in my whole life! Did I ever thank you? I am so happy, and it is all because of you!"

Jesus looked up. "Hello, Rachel. Who have you brought with you?" He turned to the many mothers who were approaching with their children. But before the group could reach Jesus, the disciples stepped in.

"Jesus is very hot and tired," one of the disciples said rudely.

"And he is hungry and needs a rest," another added. "Jesus does not have time for all these children. Why don't you all go home and leave him alone?"

Now Jesus, who was usually very kind and understanding, spoke sternly to the disciples "Let the children come to me. Don't stop them, because the kingdom of God belongs to those like them. Anyone who will not receive the kingdom of God like a little child will never enter it."

Then he took the children in his arms and blessed them. Not one person got left out that day. Jesus blessed each child who was brought to him. He loved them and listened to them. Many troubled children shared their problems with Jesus and found, to their amazement, that he already knew all about them. More importantly, he truly cared.

Levi was standing nearby with his mother. He couldn't see but listened very closely to everything that was going on around him. Suddenly, Levi sensed that Jesus was standing right by him. Would Jesus heal him? Faith grew in his young heart. *Yes, he will! I know he will!*

"Levi!" called Jesus.

Levi was startled. "You know my name?"

Jesus took him by the hand and said, "Levi, I know all about you. I knew you before you were born, I know what has happened in your life, and I even know what will happen in your future. Today, Levi, you will receive a miracle. You will be able to see again!" With that, Jesus gently touched his eyes.

"I can see! I can see!" Levi suddenly shouted. "How beautiful the world is! I can see the sky, the birds, and the trees!" He ran back to his mother and gazed at her face. "Mother, I can see you!" He turned and ran to Jesus and looked right into his warm, loving eyes. He knew he was looking into the eyes of God. "Thank you, oh, thank you, Jesus!" he exclaimed with tears running down his cheeks.

Wiping his eyes with the back of his sleeve, Levi smiled at Jesus one more time, then ran off with his friends, matching their faces with the voices he knew so well.

Word of the miracle got around quickly, and everyone came to meet the blind child who could now see.

As the whole village gathered, the women brought out the goodies that they had prepared. Everyone ate and laughed. It was the perfect end to that wonderful day. After the picnic was over, Jesus and his disciples left, smiling and waving good-bye to their new friends. The children stood there waving until he was out of sight.

The last ones to leave were Rebecca and Levi—two friends whose lives would never be the same, because they met Jesus.

Because of Jesus, Rebecca and Levi were changed forever. Not only did Jesus heal the children physically, but he did something even greater. He gave them hope for the future—a future they would not have had without Jesus' healing touch. Jesus knows all about you too, and he wants to give you a bright future and the hope of being with him in heaven someday!

The story of Jesus welcoming the children can be found in the Bible in Mark 10.

"For I know the plans I have for you," declares the Lord, "plans to prosper you and not to harm you, plans to give you hope and a future." Jeremiah 29:11 NIV

A Lunch with Jesus

Can you imagine what it might have been like to walk and talk with Jesus?
Here is a story about a little boy who truly wanted to meet Jesus face-to-face.
And in our story, that is just what happened!

The sun streamed through the window near the bed, waking Samuel from his sleep. Stretching, he smiled almost before he remembered why. He was going swimming with his friends, and today was already warm and sunny. Maybe they could stay out all day! He dragged his fingers through his dark, curly hair and went to find his mother to ask her to make him a picnic lunch.

"Now, Sam," his mother instructed him as she folded his lunch into a small cloth bundle, "don't forget to eat your lunch. Here are five small loaves and two fish. I have made them just as you like them. The fish are crisp and the loaves are warm and fresh." She kissed him good-bye and turned back into the house. Sam could hear the twins laughing and the baby starting to fuss.

Some people would consider Sam's family poor, but he never felt that way. His father and mother worked hard, but they always had enough food on the table and enjoyed being together as a family. There were so many things to be thankful to God for.

Lake Galilee was beautiful that morning. On stormy days, Sam had seen the water boil like in his mother's cooking pot. Many times, a sudden squall could change a beautiful day into a dark and dismal one. But not today! This day was perfect! The wind hardly made a ruffle on the sheet of shining water.

They had been swimming for quite a while, when they suddenly looked up and saw a boat approaching. It was just a regular fishing boat, but the men inside weren't fishing.

Isaac shouted, "Look, Sam, one of the men in the boat looks like that man, Jesus!"

They all swam to shallow water where they could stand and watch. By this time, the boat was near to shore, and they could see the men on board clearly. "It's him! It is Jesus!" Samuel cried.

He hurried to the shore and started yelling and waving to the men in the boat. The men started laughing and waving back. Jesus was dressed the same as everyone else, but it was his smile, his eyes, his way of looking into your heart that was unmistakable. There was something special about Jesus.

Sam had been drawn to Jesus since he first had heard about him. The stories of his miracles were so amazing. Sam had seen Jesus heal a blind man and even cast out a demon from a crazy man. After the demon left, the man wasn't crazy anymore. More than anything, he wanted to grow up to be one of Jesus' disciples.

The boys helped pull the boat onto the shore. As they looked inland, they could see thousands of people headed their way. It was such a colorful picture. People of all sizes, colors, and ages were coming; some running, some walking, and some stumbling from age or illness. There were men, women, and children—all coming to see Jesus.

Jesus smiled when he saw the people, then he looked around for a place to sit so that the people could see him and hear him teach. He turned to the boys, "Come, let's go up this hill and find somewhere where we can sit." Remembering his mother's words, Samuel grabbed his lunch, and off they went, running excitedly behind Jesus.

They sat down in a beautiful field. There were many trees for shade, and the many people following Jesus sat down where they could. When they were all gathered together, the grass was almost completely hidden under the mob of people.

Sam was so happy that he could hardly contain himself. He was sitting right beside Jesus! While the large crowd was finding places to sit, Jesus had talked to him, smiled at him, and asked him about his family—he had even hugged him! *This has to be the best day of my life*, he thought to himself.

Children, can you imagine yourself sitting next to Jesus?
Would you be shy, or would you ask him all the questions
you always wanted to ask him?

After a while, Jesus stood up and headed for those that were sick. Samuel never took his eyes off Jesus. However, after a while, Jesus disappeared into the crowd where none of the boys could see him.

"Where did he go?" asked Elias, looking around anxiously.

"He's gone in the direction of all of those sick people," replied Adam.

"How can Jesus touch all those people?" Jorum shook his head in wonder. "I'd be afraid I'd catch their diseases!"

The boys all looked at Sam, expecting an explanation. Sam didn't answer right away. He looked very thoughtful. "Jesus loves people," Sam answered after a while. "He loves them so much, and he wants to help them."

Just then, they heard a man yell, "I have been healed! I'm well!"

Moments later, a woman's voice cried out, "Oh thank you, Jesus! Thank you for healing my little boy!"

After a long while, Jesus came back and sat with the crowd and taught them many things. He taught about God. He taught how they should live. He taught about loving others.

The day grew cooler as the sun started its downward path. In the background, the boys overheard the disciples arguing among themselves.

"Jesus needs to send the people away. It is getting late, and there's no food for them," Philip said.

Jesus overheard and answered him, "Where can we buy bread for all of these people to eat?"

Philip answered him: "Eight months' of pay wouldn't buy enough bread for everyone to have a bite!"

Sam leaned over and quietly handed his little bundle of food to one of the disciples. The man spoke up. "There is a boy with five small barley loaves and two small fish, but how far will they go among so many?"

Jesus looked right in Sam's eyes and smiled. Samuel was happy to have pleased Jesus.

"Have the people sit down in small groups," Jesus directed the disciples. He then looked toward heaven, gave thanks, and broke the loaves. Then he gave the pieces of bread to the disciples, and the disciples gave them to the people. He kept breaking off pieces and putting them in baskets for the disciples. With every basket filled, Sam's amazement grew.

The other boys began to talk excitedly among themselves. "Can you believe that?!" one of his friends cried. "Your small lunch has fed everyone! Jesus has fed the biggest crowd that I have ever seen. What a miracle!"

They even had leftovers! After everyone finished eating, there were twelve baskets of fish and bread left over. Jesus gave one of the baskets to Samuel and his friends, and that basket alone had far more food in it than Sam's little lunch had to start with.

Something changed for Samuel that day. He now had friends that believed in Jesus the way he did. And from that time on, they talked about Jesus the Messiah whenever they played together. Sam knew he would follow Jesus for the rest of his life!

I know there are times when we think we have nothing we can give to Jesus. At other times, we may think what we have is too small. But look what happened when a little boy shared his lunch with Jesus!

What gifts or talents do you have that can be used for Jesus?

If you would like to read more about this story in the Bible, go to John 6:1–15

The Little Lost Lamb

*It makes me laugh when I see the fluffy, white lambs
running and playing together in the fields.*

*Even though animals and humans don't speak the same language,
we can communicate. Do you have a dog or a cat? If so, you and your pet
probably communicate without talking. I am sure you know what they are
saying when they look at you a certain way and make a familiar sound.
And they know what you're saying when you pet them and hug them tight.*

*Jesus told a story about a shepherd who loved each of his sheep
and knew them very well. But one day, a little lamb was lost. . . .*

Many years ago, in the land of Israel, there lived a wonderful, loving shepherd. His sheep roamed some beautiful fields with lots of tasty, green grass, colorful flowers, and a clear stream of cold, fresh water. The shepherd knew each of his sheep by name, and he knew how to protect them from the wolves and bears that were always looking for a tasty meal!

Guess how many sheep and lambs the shepherd had? One hundred! What would you do with that many animals in one place? Just think about the noise they must have made, when all of them together said, "Baaaaaaa."

The shepherd had only one rule: the sheep were never to leave their field. Every evening as he gathered them into the fold, and every morning as he let them out to graze, this good shepherd counted his sheep. One morning, the shepherd counted his one hundred sheep and sent them off to eat and play. The sun was shining brightly; it was not too hot and not too cold. A warm breeze tickled the ears of the little lambs.

When evening came, the shepherd counted his sheep. A puzzled look came over his face, and he counted them again. "Oh no!" he said to himself. "I had better count them again!" He again counted to ninety-nine, and there were no more sheep to be found.

The sheep whispered among themselves, "What is going on?"

The shepherd knew instantly that it was Rafi that was missing. He turned to the other sheep and said, "I must go find my little lamb and bring him safely home." And off the good shepherd went, leaving his ninety-nine sheep, to look for one rebellious, lost lamb!

Rafi had ventured away from the rest of the sheep when no one was looking. "I am free! No one can tell me where to go or what to do. This is going to be *fun*!"

He leapt over bushes and chased butterflies until he realized he was lost!

When the shadows were long and the sun was almost gone, Rafi heard the low growl of wolves that lived in a nearby cave. He shuddered. In the growing darkness, he thought he could see the glint of eyes looking at him from behind a nearby bush.

He froze and tried to be invisible. "I want my mommy. . . . I want my shepherd," he cried to himself.

"I don't want to be the wolves' dinner!" Rafi bleated. He started to run down the mountain trail. The sharp rocks cut into his hooves and the rough brambles tore at his soft fleece. He tripped on a loose rock and tumbled head over heels. Down he rolled, faster and faster.

Down and down he went until he landed in a heap at the bottom of the mountain.

Meanwhile, the shepherd had been searching in the darkness. "Rafi," he shouted desperately, but there was no reply. After hours and hours, the shepherd began to hear noises that he recognized but did not like. He bravely followed the sound of a wolf stalking his prey, knowing he would probably find his lamb there.

Don't you think the shepherd was very brave to face the wolves in order to protect his little lamb?

Rafi heard the scratching of claws on dirt and the crunching of leaves. *If only I had obeyed the shepherd*, he thought. *He would have kept me safe*. The wolves came nearer and nearer.

The smallest sound of a voice in the distance made Rafi lift up his head. He heard it again, louder this time. It was his shepherd's voice calling his name! Rafi tried to bleat, but he was so weak, the first try didn't make it past his dry lips. He tried again, and a small, muffled sound came out. But it was enough. The shepherd heard it. He knew his sheep. He knew them when they were strong and loud, and he knew them when they were weak and afraid. He ran to the lost lamb.

Solar System

"Solar" means "of the sun."

A solar system includes all the planets and natural satellites that orbit a sun (star). Our own Solar System includes:

- **The Sun**
- **8 planets: in order from the Sun:** Mercury, Venus, Earth, Mars, Jupiter, Saturn, Uranus, Neptune
- **5 dwarf planets:** Ceres, Pluto, Haumea, Makemake, Eris
- **Many moons, meteors, comets, asteroids, and interplanetary (between planets) dust**

Exploring the Solar System

The Soviet space probe **Venera 7** made a controlled landing on Venus in 1970.

In 1972, NASA launched **Pioneer 10**, the first space probe to travel to outer planets.

NASA's spacecraft **Voyager I** was launched in 1977 to explore our Solar System. Thirty years later, it reached its very edge.

In 2001, **NEAR Shoemaker** was the first space probe to land on an asteroid, Eros.

The wolves eyed their future dinner: a chunky, lost lamb. They crouched down, ready to pounce when they heard an unwelcome sound. It was the voice of the strong shepherd. Just weeks before, that same shepherd had struck their snouts with his staff, and it hurt! The wolves thought it best to go without dinner and skulked off, disappointed.

The shepherd found the pitiful little heap of dirty wool that was his lost lamb. He knelt beside Rafi, putting a soothing hand on the wooly head. Rafi looked into the face of the shepherd and saw two things: the tears streaming down his face and the beautiful smile Rafi knew so well. The shepherd picked him up, hugged him gently, and carried him home.

I will never leave the flock again, Rafi thought. *I have everything I need and more. I have the best shepherd in the world. He loves me even when I wander, he looks for me when I'm lost, and he cares for me when I'm hurt.*

Rafi and the shepherd came over the hill by the field just as the sun rose. All the sheep were so happy! "Rafi's home! He's home!"

After that, the sheep would tell Rafi's story whenever a new sheep would join the flock—how the shepherd had left the fold of ninety-nine sheep to look for the one that was lost.

Why do you think Rafi wished he had followed the shepherd's rules?
Have you ever wished you had chosen to follow
one of your parents' rules?
Sometimes not following the rules can cause us serious problems!
Rafi was nearly wolves' dinner because he didn't obey the shepherd.

Who does the shepherd remind you of? That's right, Jesus.
Jesus loves us no matter what we do. He has also given us rules
to help us stay safe and happy. Where can we find his rules?

Jesus' parable of the shepherd can be found in the Bible in Luke 15:3–7.

The Butterfly and the Cross

Have you ever seen a butterfly floating through the air in the springtime, flying from flower to flower, as lightly as a soap bubble?

Do you know that God created many different kinds of butterflies? Some are as tiny as your little fingernail. The Queen Alexandra butterfly is the largest kind of butterfly in the world. When her wings are spread open, they are as wide your two hands!

You can find butterflies in most parts of the world, whether it is warm or cold, dry or moist, hilly or flat. I'm sure you're not surprised to know that some butterflies make their homes in Israel, where Jesus lived.

Once upon a time near Jerusalem, there lived a very beautiful butterfly named Alexandra. She was a stunning yellow, almost golden color, and she had striking brown markings on her delicate wings. She loved to find the tastiest flowers and drink the nectar with her long tongue, like you would drink a milkshake with a straw.

On this day, a breeze was making the flowers sway, as if they were dancing along with the sparrow's song. Most butterflies have to watch out for birds, but Alex was bigger than the sparrows, so she didn't give them a second thought. High, high on the breeze, Alexandra floated and played.

As she flew, she saw the fuzzy, little caterpillars feasting on the green leaves of a small bush. "Miss Alex, come tell us a story," they cried. Alex stopped for a moment and told them of a miracle that the man Jesus, had done. Alex was amazed each time she heard news of Jesus and loved sharing the stories with the young caterpillars.

As Alex waved good-bye to the caterpillars, she noticed something odd: the air was too still. Her heart beat faster. "Something's wrong—something bad is about to happen," she feared.

You see, all of God's creatures are very sensitive to the world around them. Do you know that when a tidal wave is coming, all creatures— dogs, sheep, horses, cattle, and even sand crabs—run up into the hills? They sense trouble is coming, and out of harm's way they go.

Usually the butterflies were very chatty, but today each one became more and more silent. "You feel it too, don't you?" Alex asked her friends. They all twitched their feelers and fluttered their wings in agreement.

Although it was still, it wasn't quiet. There was a strange sound coming from the city. It was the sounds of humans. Some were shouting, some were screaming, and some were crying.

The sounds became louder now, and out of the city came a huge crowd of people. Everyone was watching one man—a man carrying a wooden thing, almost like a tree. He looked as if he'd been beaten.

The business of humans usually is of little interest to butterflies, but on this day, the butterflies took notice of the crowd. The butterflies flew closer to the hill called Golgotha.

"Look!" cried a Tiger butterfly. "That is the man called Jesus. I once saw him heal a man whose legs didn't work."

"I saw him fix the eyes of a blind man," said another.

"That's the one who brought the dead man back to life!" Alex said triumphantly. No one had believed her when she'd told them that story.

Jesus reached the top of the hill, and the butterflies watched helplessly as angry people hung him on the cross-shaped wood. She could see the ugly nails in his feet and hands. Drawn by something she didn't understand, Alexandra fluttered her wings and floated toward the hill.

"Come back, Alex. It's not safe!" called her frightened friends.

She flew to his right hand and landed on the cross. She looked into Jesus' face, and all she could see was an expression of love. She couldn't believe that this man, who had done nothing wrong, could love even the people who hurt him.

I don't understand everything that goes on with humans, but I know that there is no one like this man, she thought.

She could tell that he was going to die. "You are indeed a king," she whispered to Jesus.

Alexandra started to fly back to safety but found that she couldn't move. The bottom tip of one of her delicate wings was stuck under a long splinter of the rough wood. She struggled to get free. Alex was so afraid! Would she die too?

In answer to her fear, a single drop of blood ran down from one of Jesus' hands and fell on her trapped wing. The blood loosened her wing and set her free. She soared into the air.

Alexandra took one look back as Jesus died. Darkness came over the whole land. The sun stopped shining. The earth shuddered, knocking the soldiers on the hill off of their feet. Cries of fear went up from the city, and the curtain in the temple was miraculously torn in two.

Alex slowly flew home.

"What happened to you?" her friends asked when she arrived.

"I was with Jesus and was caught and his blood freed me," she told them breathlessly.

"Look at you," they said. "You're different!"

And she was. The most extraordinary red and purple colors had been added to the brown and yellow of her wings. Jesus' blood had become a permanent reminder of how God's own Son had set her free. It was magnificent!

So, children, what about you? Jesus died on the cross that day for all of our sins, and just as the butterfly was freed by the blood, Jesus' blood sets us free—but in a different way. It sets us free from our sins, which separate us from God.

You see, we all have sinned. Every one of us has done wrong and deserves a punishment. Jesus never sinned, yet he took the punishment for our sins. And if we accept him, we don't have to pay the penalty. We are free forever to live with God in heaven after we die.

Would you like to tell Jesus today that you love him, trust him,
and give your heart to him?
All you have to do is to ask him to forgive your sins, and he'll do it!
Isn't it a wonderful gift?
He died so that we could live!

The story of Jesus' crucifixion can be found in John 18–19.

Here is a scripture for you to remember:
For God so loved the world that he gave his one and only Son,
that whoever believes in him shall not perish but have eternal life.
John 3:16 NIV